Wounds of the Old Trees

Iraqi Poems

Sadiq Assaieg
Translated and Edited by Soheil Najm

Plain View Press
P.O. 42255
Austin, TX 78704

plainviewpress.net
pk@plainviewpress.net
512-441-2452

Copyright © 2011 Sadiq Assaieg. All rights reserved under International and Pan-American Copyright Conventions. No part of this book may be reproduced or distributed in any form or by any means, or stored in a data base or retrieval system, without written permission from the author. All rights, including electronic, are reserved by the author and publisher.

ISBN: 978-1-935514-18-3
Library of Congress Control Number: 2011929484

Cover art by Sadiq Assaieg
Cover design by Sherry L. Pilisko

Also by Sadiq Assaieg:
The Song of Rhinoceros, Baghdad 1978; *A Country for the Soul*, Beirut; *The Place of the Heart*, Beirut; *Flying of Long Distances*, Beirut; *I Am the Dust*, Baghdad-Damascus; *A Stone Crying*, Baghdad-Damascus; *The Poems of Love*, Baghdad-Damascus; *The Poems of Isolation*, Baghdad, Damascus.

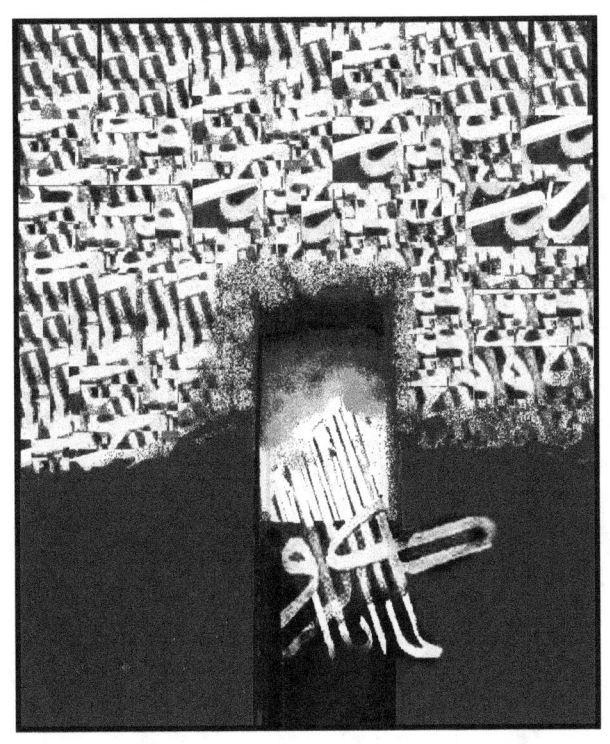

Artwork by Sadiq Assaieg

Contents

Under the Sky of Stockholm	9
A Dream	10
Your Ideal Icon	11
In the Apple Garden	12
Ophelia	13
Sargon Bolous	14
You Were Born in the Sky	15
With All Your Mistakes!	17
The Agonies of the Prophets	18
Without a Guide	19
Towards the Heart	20
Like a Little Puppy	21
With a Cut Pharynx	22
In Treadless Roads	23
Flying Through Long Distances	24
As the Birds Escape	26
Where Nobody Cares	27
The Place of the Wounds	28
Is There Any Use	29
From Place to Another	30
The Second Versant of the Mountain	31
Impossible	33
Mud Throb	34
The Day When You Flow Over With Your Soul	35
A Lonely Wave	36
An Enormous Heart	37
The Old Tree	38
Forget What I Meant	39
Towards a Flash Light	40
Perfumes	41
The Black Angel	42
I Love You	43
Sparrows of Depress	44

Towards a White Direction	45
Laugh	46
Return from Another Place	47
By the Teeth of the Ploughs	48
The Scarecrow	49
Help	50
Smoke of Sorry	51
The Orchid Flower	52
Nobody Will Find You	53
The Child	55
I Am the Dust	57
Humming	58
A Black God	59
I Lost You	60
The Corruption of Truths	61
Blockade	62
A Far Away Land	63
Mountains	64
To Bottomless	65
This Is Baghdad	66
The Most Beautiful Woman in the World	71
The Iraqis	72
Helicopters of Schwarzkopf	73
Helicopters	74
'Til the End of the World	75
Portrait	77
The Eyes of Foxes	78
In One Kiss	79
Lift Me as a Rose	80
From Love…From Loneliness	81
Let Not the Wolf Enter the Garden of Your House	82
About the Author	87
About the Translator and Editor	89

Artwork by Sadiq Assaieg

Under the Sky of Stockholm

A fanciful bell
hanging in the space.
I throw a stone at it
when I heard vibrations
echoing
your name.

A Dream

You and me
were in a wood.
You said:
"Close your eyes".
And I closed my eyes
And let us disappear.

As if in a dream,
as if in death
I stretched my hand to the darkness and said:
"O my love
I see you
can you see me?"

The trees
with their human limbs
were rippling,
your hair behind the stems
were rippling.
Even the music was rippling.

And as in dream,
as in death
with my closed eyes I hear you saying:
"O my beloved
I am a sick child
so embrace me to recover."

Behind vibrations I couldn't see them,
behind colors I couldn't see them too
And fresh breeze
I was running after you,
like a wave,
with closed eyes saying:
"O my beloved
I can see you,
can you see me?"

Your Ideal Icon

Your ideal example,
your half statue,
your beautiful example
with great languages
will appear on TV after a while
to change his skin,
to metamorphose into a lizard.

He will cry
asking your forgiveness.

Your ideal example
will take off his skin
and his old bones
to take a nap on the sands
taking a bath
under a warm sun!

In the Apple Garden

I came out without weight,
sticking to the wind
sands throwing me here and there.

Yet God was watching the scene
on his lips a happy smile.

Ophelia

Under a dark sun
a flock of crazy flies
fly low
over the water
looking for Ophelia's head.

When she,
in the charming of a floating flower,
harmonizes with her loneliness
up and down
runs with the stream,
surrenders to the sunset,
to the trees of the road
and to the choir of the angels
playing for her
from nowhere.

Sargon Bolous[1]

Sargon,
you who is the root of poetry and loses,
you whose eyes stray
for thousands of years
in the pain mills,
you can now
listen, as you used to,
to what the winds say
to a fragile branch.

Sargon,
let your poems blaze
flowers
scattering in the heart of the sky
complimenting your luminous pain

Throw, prince of poetry and loses,
your burdens outside the space
and interest seeing them fly
in its wide beautiful depth.

In a kick from the heel of your shoe
get away from time limits
as a silk shawl
or as a bright shiny moment
or a piece of music
among the colors of the clouds.

In the softness of sleep and illness
and a smile about to recover
with a last love song
you'll reach to that wide world
that let you in
at last.

---

[1] Sargon Bolous (1944 – October 22, 2007), an Iraqi Assyrian poet, translator and short story writer.

You Were Born in the Sky

They said
after you had died
your soul would ascend to the sky
and pain would reveal.

They said
with a hit of a sword
your head alone,
like a colored balloon,
would ascend trotting
exulted
in its magic ringing.

Like a light boat
in your oars and music
the wind will raise you
higher and higher
till the marks will
disappear
and you'll be separated from
your tears,
your years,
you're past and present
When the earth beneath you
shackled by chains.

They said,
Sargon,
you are there
born in the sky,

in the cage of God,
whenever he heard the creak of the doors
and the rattle of the locks
his color changes
and become
dry grass.

Hurriedly he crosses the street
accompanied with long ghosts
and whenever he hastens
they move faster than him.

Sawdust and ash
whistle hard
in the panels,
in the low windows
and the electric cables.

Oh for these guesses
in such bad weather!
He says to himself,
oh for these guesses!

Here he is
accompanied with his ghosts,
returns again
to cross spirally
the street
like a smoke column.

With All Your Mistakes!

It happens sometimes
that you leave your body
walking in the rooms
like a roaming internal torch,
like a watch ticking,
like an animal its soul in a cage
thinking
in confusing things, like
"The cooling of blood",
"The heating of air"
and "the explosion of the brain"

But now you are
like a white smoking liquid,
one day
by the activity of the senses
and a sudden sparkle
you'll explode
with all your mistakes!

The Agonies of the Prophets

The prophet said his word
and disappeared in the smoke.

The earth was issuing
suppressed moaning
in behalf of a little God
whose soul in flame
and his body burned by the cigarettes
for unlimited time.
alone he will be left in this grave
no one to close his eyelids
nor his tired heart
will stop throbbing.

The prophet said his word
and disappeared in the smoke.

Without a Guide

If you are lucky
you will find God
inside a tiny atom.
You'll find yourself
inside its map
alive
enlightening
and you will breathe freely
without a guide.

Towards the Heart

The black Mercedes
with its front high light
crept slowly
towards a tiny object,
towards a heart thrown on the asphalt
to smash it,
to smash by its wheels
the remains of an old love.

Like a Little Puppy

The clouds with bells
dropped my flamed water
among forbidden fruits.
So I went deep
in fruitful turnings
that led my thirsty soul
to smooth skin
soaked
with drops of gold.

The clouds with bells
took me
to a blazed wound
latent
in the darkness of the pelvis
among the shadows of the branches.

There
I fluttered and fluttered,
moaning and kneeling
turning and pleading
like a little puppy.

With a Cut Pharynx

I will go out
of here,
from one of the houses
to say good bye to these banks
these last banks
to send the last signs
to the other side of the city.

I'll go out
with a colorful bead in my chest,
a spot of blood
and a knocked down heart.

I'll go out
hardly breathe
to die many times,
to lay
and catch my cut pharynx
to relax at last
sensing the humidity of the earth
throbbing on the grass
like a big geranium.

In Treadless Roads

Hey hungry city
this is the Iraqi, your son,
your animal that was born in your womb
like a black spot.
Here he is

sneaking at night
in the treadles roads,
hiding like a ghost
to change his appearance,
to neigh,
to search for your soul and his
in the debris of the wars.

Flying Through Long Distances

Come,
let us fly with the snow
to be scraped off by the winds
incessantly.

Come to ascend,
to run on the slopes of the horizon
on the extension of the walls
where the storms
ascend.

Come
towards the high summits,
towards exuberant spaces,
towards far away distances
where the moon
with her agitated emotions
and her variegated scars
crosses the woods
with the streams
for new unknowns and spaces.

Come
to the flying of the winds
with spirits float in the air,
with the angels,
with the silk scarves,
with the paradises,
with the Ursa Minor,
with the unknown,
with...with...
till the end.

Come,
let us mix with the spectrums
and ascend to invisible paradises
where little exulting drops of blood
mix with the shining clouds
glaring
and wet in the drizzle.

As the Birds Escape

In order to die I'll go to the sea.

I'll escape
to a save place
as the birds do.

I'll run and run
towards those far away fields
till my soul fall
in a blind hole.

Where Nobody Cares

The seasons decrease
and so are we.

We will never go home this time.

Mysterious winds
will take us
towards those fields,
towards a hidden night
its jets flow in the darkness
and its bells—they said—
play
during our slumber.

The Place of the Wounds

In this blue night
magnetized by
the falls of isolation
you wake up
with a thirsty mouth
and small countless tortures.

Like an old tree
you stretch out your fingers
towards the pain that limed
and feel
the place of the wounds.

Is There Any Use

to Najeeb Almanie[2]

What else if you smelt the Aden lower
and slumbered?
Did you alert by the surprise?
Did you feel different?

When you rested your head
and slumbered
at the sound of the blue Danube
did you lose your memory?
Did you feel the movement in the curtains,
the breeze blow up on you
from the other coast?
From the other side of life?

Are you going to turn around,
to wave to anybody?
Is this your last word?
Are we going to meet again?
Or the earth will collect you
as it collects its scattered papers?

Najeeb,
Is there any use?

---

2   Najeeb Almanie, Iraqi novelist, critic and translator (1926- 1982).

From Place to Another

For Badr Shakir Asseiab[3]

We will remain listening
to the fall of the water
where there are neither tabs,
nor jars.

We will only listen
to the mew of the black cats
hanging on in the dim darkness
dragging with their claws
the veins of the heart
from place to another.

---

3   Badr Shakir Asseiab, Iraqi and Arab poet (December 24, 1926–1964). Asseiab with his colleagues al-Bayati, al-Haidery and Nazik al-Malaika were the pioneers of Iraqi and Arab modern poetry who defied the conventional form of Arabic poetry that had been common for centuries.

The Second Versant of the Mountain

In that place
we were multiplying
like little multiplication tables.
We were written
and erased
and run in the turnings.

By the singing of the wind
we were drying the washing.

Every one of us
was perching on the wires like a bird,
very proud of his stubbornness,
rubbing his wings
by the electricity pillars.

One day,
in a vague way,
we passed the fifties,
we climbed high roads
going up to the turnings
then going down
to the second versant of the
mountain.

There,
we returned
to the way we already passed through,
to our childhood
to our white days,
to our scattered bags
and our bikes leaned
on the second versant of the mountain.

There
our hearts were throbbing,
our looks were strange
and there was
a little bird
very proud of his stubbornness,
boasting of
rubbing his wings
by the electricity pillars.

Impossible

A slim light
senses the earth
knowing
that his task is impossible.
Every time
it clashes with dislocated yells,
with silent hearts
their blood dried
on the fences and the walls.

And every time
it draws back
to its total whiteness
where the agonies are covered
with the cover of snow
and oblivion.

Mud Throb

> to Buland al-Haidery[4]

Your beautiful heart
will be erased
and will never shine again.

Your heart
will ascend to heaven
never knows any kind of light that touches it,
never knows what happens
in those far away distances
nor what happens
in that bewitched emptiness.

Your heart
will go for its affair
ablaze,
shining
launching its friendly signs
melting in its heaven
as the sugar does.

Your heart
in its exuberant skies
will remain awake
enchanted by its death,
by its beauty,
by the beauty of that strange hand
that stretched out
to pick it up
and take it for ever
like a hot lemon
to its last ease.

---

4   Buland al-Haidery, Iraqi poet (1926–September 26, 1996).

The Day When You Flow Over With Your Soul

You were happy then
and your mother was calling you
as she was calling
a bird on the tree.

You were singing
alone
as if you were
apart from the darkness.

One day
you flow over with your soul,
recoiled
and for mysterious reasons,
scrupulous is one of them,
captivated
by strange visions
You left in winter day,
didn't care neither by the bad climate
nor the calls of your mother,
nor
the angry thunderclap
among the branches.

A Lonely Wave

A single wave
resisting the stream.
Its broken mouth yells
over the rocks.

A wave we left alone
and it will be eaten
alone.

An Enormous Heart

I astonish for this great rock
it sits in the sun
all the day
never complaining,
never cracking,
nor exploding
like an enormous heart.

The Old Tree

This old tree
could not count its leaves any more,
nor does it want to give
a new proof.

It is enough for it to feed
on little talk,
it is enough for it to remember
that time
doesn't turn back
nor cares
about the passengers.

Forget What I Meant

Don't be afraid oh heart,
I say.
Sink in the water
to the bottom
in the deep ether
and let the ghosts
outside
fighting each other alone.

Forget oh heart your words,
forget the meaning,
forget what I meant,
forget your weight,
forget the earth and magnetism
and sink
in a tiny drop of water,
it too,
swims in a transparent light.

Towards a Flash Light

Nothing.
Nothing
changes the direction of the edge
but its internal silence,
but
stones and broken bottles
fall
from the holes
to the deep valleys of his heart.

Nothing
but frightened birds
their shocked flocks
rush to the horizon
towards the clouds.

Perfumes

He will let his key turn
in her sleeping heart
permitting his ray
slips into her body
loaded with domes
and into her narrow banks
soaked with love water.

He will let her feel
overwhelmed
by endless tranquility
and wet
by all the perfumes of the world.

The Black Angel

In the dark room
a black flower
illuminating the walls and the sheets
and there was a black angel
roosting on the chest of the sleeping man.

With metal eyes
and feverish breaths
the angel bends
gazes at the man's eyes
without saying a word.

I Love You

This night
you'll find me dead between your arms
and many people
talk inside me.

You'll identify me
from my pains
and from black shadows
around the lashes
and below the eyes.

You'll find my soul
empty from sunlight
like an image of a dead man
and many people talk
inside him.

Sparrows of Depress

This night
I lay on the depress bed
little sparrows come out of my tears
leaving smashed flowers
beneath the eyelids.

We became strangers,
I said
and you said:
This type of illusions,
this type of depress.

Yesterday
I stared in your face,
I explored your smile
to the sun shine
and said:
I am useless
and you resemble me for sure.

We became strangers,
lately,
exchanging loosing words
laughing sadly
and then hang up the phone.

Everything changes pretty girl,
hurriedly changes
and from all the colors
small stars collect,
tormented stars,
bursting tears in our eyes.

Towards a White Direction

to Abdul-Wahab al-Bayati[5]

Towards a white direction
no body heads for
I walked halve of the way to Hajj
halve of the way to the end
and said:
My God,
this is my last flight,
save me!

But,
because of the earth magnetism
my words were slow
mumbled
fatigued
unable to fly,
my words had gone
taken with them
my fever,
my poems
and the last call.

---

5   Abdul-Wahab al-Bayati, Iraqi poet (1926–1999).

Laugh

O death,
one day
I'll climb your nest
free and happy
like the sunlight,

I'll surprise you death
with my simple words
and my white poems.

And as in the past
we will stay loyal
kidding,
making toasts
and laugh as friends.

We will laugh much my friend
laugh
and laugh
till our laugh changes into
flame
into tremor,
into death
into weep.

Return from Another Place

A skeleton
stands in dim light
turning around with tens of shadows

wondering:
Is this the place?
Do I lose the way?
Is there any way?
Do I imagine?
Do I hear somebody calling me personally?
I am sure I imagined that
and I should return
from another place.

By the Teeth of the Ploughs

Agony
resists you
be tenacious to the winds
and to the teeth of the ploughs.

Agony
against you,
against fire,
against the wind
competing with you
and interrupt your way.

Agony
leaves you asleep on the stones
and stay
awake
shining
below the eyelids.

The Scarecrow

I am the scarecrow
nobody sees me,
nobody talks to me
because I am dead
and my clothes
are wet by the rain.

I see death roosting
among the shadows of the trees
and among the left bones.
I see a tuft from woman's hair
and a child's head
slaughtered with a knife.

I see gleaming blades
their spiral elegance
crosses the limits,
I see soldiers
their troops
heading forward
to fasten the flags on the summits.
Then
in the explosion of the sun
their smoke goes up
in the sky.

Beneath skies
fill of shining spiders I have been killed.
I am now just a dead staff of grass
nobody sees me
I see nobody
and the rains wet my clothes.

Help

Whenever I shouted:
Help,
the door was closed
and a red fire was ignited.

I have a thousand arms,
I believe in God
and correctly I count the numbers
1+1=51
02-1=59

But what is the use
as long as I am dead
and nobody hears my shouting.

Smoke of Sorry

I was a child,
so I wrote my dream
on the side of a small boat.
I colored it
with green chalk
and launched it
towards the waves.

Now
I wake up
to see a white smoke
coming up from that boat
and my soul
coming up from another earth.

It is the
smoke of sorry
slowly goes out,
stings,
bitter
and stick to the pharynx.

The Orchid Flower

A little drop of blood
from my cut off lips
fall on your back
and
went down
to the other side
of the orchid flower.

A drop of blood
soaked by alcohol
slipped
on a soft delicate skin
not knowing
why its breaths were cut
and its waves were high
drifted by storm
almost pushing ahead
towards the estuary.

Nobody Will Find You

one who leaves the country he lives in will never be happy.
—Milan Condera

The Hard Crossing:
The distance appears short, for the first time,
but it is too long and gross!!
Cavavis

Where will you travel?
Traveling in this age is too slow.
Every mile of pain
needs a whole day.

You'll never know
if you go or back,
if you a victorious or a loser.
Is this your ship landing at a coast
or this is your wreck
landing at the harbor?

You'll never know
how suddenly you get old!
how the waves of the age have broken!
How your fire extinguished!
And you will wonder,
Was that a dream?
Was that you
or just a passerby?

As if you didn't expect
a man with a black cloak
would knock your door,
you were kidding with him as a friend
and play chess with him.
Here he comes
to finish with you
in one move
a postpone game
the circumstances postponed it
till now.

The day you will decide to return,
traces will have been gone
and the signs will have been changed
and it will be too late
for anybody to find you.

The Child

When he reappeared
nobody was there.
There was no time,
there was no watch,
nor pointers,
nor a witness around,
nor anyone to proof.
what you have seen
whether it was you
or another child.

You were standing at your balcony
listening to the memories,
launching their mysterious moaning,
throwing the last looks on the world
when the child appeared
lifted by the wings of the wind
between the way and the forest.

Since he waved to you
wave and smile.
You waved and smiled
and descended your balcony having fever.
You hurriedly came down the stairs
holding your bleeding wound
looking for it everywhere,
in the turnings
and between the way and the forest.
then you stopped
sending out long and lost sights
through the passages and paths.

The child had gone
leaving on the fence
a white handkerchief,
remains of breaths
and a sun setting
among the stems.

No one was there,
neither time
nor numbers,
nor a watch,
nor even a person to witness.
Whether you saw
a real child
or just a fancy wind movement
never happened
among the trees.

I Am the Dust

I am the dust
my bones agitate
by your breaths.

Humming

Old repentance,
you never know its source.
Its mouth is open,
its eyes halve closed.
Look like a rusty tool.
Suddenly explodes
to bite your bowels
and your cries
leaving your heart
variegated with holes.

A Black God

A black god
silently smokes
and waits you
among the trees.

He will walk beside you
down road
putting his hand on your shoulder
taking you out of the world
to an unknown direction
where the curtains let down
and all the lights put out.

I Lost You

Just two steps away from the house
I lost my way,
I lost you.

The Corruption of Truths

"I am not the same person
now, oh Eve", he told her.
"I prefer my blindness
to anything else".

"Miss, forget the story of Adam and Eve",
He told her,
"Forget everything".

"I'd better kill you", he told her at last.
"Because the apple killed not Adam,
oh Eve,
it was
the corruption of truths".

Blockade

A heavy bag
filled with gods.
feeling hungry
I sold it today on the pavement.

A Far Away Land

This land
on which you put your ear
neither has a heart
nor a soul.
Neither can it hear your weeping
nor the crying of the springs.

This land
could not read the codes
nor the messages buried in its lower layers.
It doesn't want to hear
the voices coming out of the vaults
nor the cries of the dead,
nor the hidden moaning
released
from the collective tombs.

This land
on which you put your ear
doesn't care about the ends
nor the proofs.

It is a cold land,
far away
and know nothing
about these agonies.

Mountains

These mountains
sleep side by side
like hunchback cats.

like us,
their eyes are red,
overburdened,
sick,
and they cannot breathe
nor can they fly.

To Bottomless

Under a dead sky
I see trees
come nearer.

I see faces
gazing at me
and hands
raising lamps against my face.

Under a dead sky
and pitch dark
I see myself
going down
and down
and down
to bottomless.

This Is Baghdad

This city is a miracle;
Bombs thrown down at it,
smashed under feet
like a broken watch,
yet,
as if reborn;
You can heard it ticking, under the debris,
you can sense its heart,
and its lost parts.

A miracle city
in a state of dreaming and delirium;
History memorizes its poems.
Its houses are ruins,
its buildings are forlorn,
yet its colored flags
surrender to the touches of April wind,
stabled on the roofs and the masts,
sewed with worn patches
designed in simple artistic sense
remain to hail the limits of agony and loss.

It throbs and gleams under the sun,
coloring the faces of the poor and the streets
with the sky colors and angels
It is a city afflicted with dreams of future.
Its body is in flame
and its faucet is dry.
There is wrath, hunger
and teeth gnashing in its depths.
A city that history,
snipers, lovers, poets,

invaders, barbarians and oil thieves are
ravenous for
in every age they thought it dead.
A very long cry erupts
from the depths of her soul,
circulates in her air like broken waves:
"To die or not to die,
to live or not to live
to be or not to be
that is the question".

Yesterday,
pupils of the preliminary school,
who had survived from one hell of a bombing,
went out of their classes to the alley,
played a long penalty kick,
That split the space like a flying dish.
Sailing over the laundry lines hung with wet clothes
To land a new disaster,
Breaking the neighbors' window.

At Abu-Ibrahim's café
Which is well known as the café of the "complicated group"
full of book lovers, poets and unemployed people,
human wind pipes come to blows in a resound debate,
this time
about a prose poem.
It's the author, who is ready to fight any one,
insisting that it is designed according to "Dadaism".
That is why it is afflicted with bird-flu virus,
no need to say that it bears a
"Suq Mureidy"[6] sign,
commented another man
bestowed with mistrust for modern art,

---

6   Suq Mureidy, A public market in Baghdad.

after he set down a domino piece,
while some others argued about
a new play described as "popular"
while some others described it as the "essence of misunderstanding"
of "pop" theory and the visual art
after the world war,
and an acute debate wave
blow up from the back row
about contents of the fourth dimension,
Ibrahim al-Jaffari[7], Fokoyama
and the end of history.

not far from the hotel
of hajj Hamoodi al-Doori,
that is well known as "The Greats' House"
at a public market
cars passed through crossing the bridge;
I saw them, in my eyes, flying,
speeding along the asphalt of the street
as if they were meteors,
a bride inside one of them,
she will lose her virginity this night,
the captain hajj Rzuqi
and the applause of the crowd people
in the shop of hajj Hamodi al-Doori,
near al-Mutanabi street,
a radio with a bad teeth sang
a song of sympathy for Zuhur Hussein[8]
then came the new broadcaster,
to apologize about a mistake in broadcasting,
and about a simple change
for the time of the news
according to Greenwich time

---

7   Ibrahim al-Jaffari, The Iraqi ex-prime minister.
8   Zuhur Hussein, Iraqi woman singer who was well known during the sixties.

and at three o'clock
exactly as the last raid was over
an Indian parrot sang in Arabic
before a crowd of children—
surrounded it—
a Ilham al-Madfaie[9] song "Mohammed oh Mohemmed."
Then it climbed in arrogance onto
an artificial green bough
delighted by its long bow tail.

Amazing city as I said.
Snipers, prophets and killers are searching for it,
angels, poets and saints.
An eastern fabulous crazy city,
with luminous crescents.
One of the most beautiful cities in the world,
Its depth is rocked by bombing everyday
without losing its balance.
Although its women
are whispering to their men in low voice at night,
lest the children wake
yet men don't hear despair,
and go on.

A miracle city
its crescents are always drunk,
and their stars are drunk too.
Although bombs are thrown at it
and it is smashed like a broken watch,
yet it stays ticking.

As if it were reborn,
risen from the garbage,
And on broken light wings—

---

9   Ilham al-Madfaie, Iraqi singer

a code for the forthcoming generations,
its heart still throbbing and throbbing
like the singing nightingale alarm of the broadcasting
ringing with all strength
with power and steadiness,
in spite of everything remain,
the words
this is Baghdad
this is Baghdad
this is Baghdad.

The Most Beautiful Woman in the World

Death will blow over me
from kind arms,
from wet breeze,
from fresh sunset
and from a pale moon.

You will be
my white flower
my poisoned killing flower
that sleeps on my tomb
pleased and happy.

With your underwear,
your bare feet
and your sly smile
under the dimly light
you'll be the most beautiful woman
in the world.

The Iraqis

The Iraqis
breathe slower than the breath of the trees,
slower than the breath of the centuries.

The Iraqis
with sinful, broken hearts,
come closer and remote
from each other
without any directions.

Helicopters of Schwarzkopf

The helicopters of Schwarzkopf
sticking to the skin
like shining insects
searching in the deed's eyes
about the ancestors' irises.

Wild helicopters
and lusty senses
crowded over the corpses
when you diffuse them they make round,
when you hit them they slip,
when you keep them off they back
to bounce down on the preys
licking the taste of blood
in the coaly races,
in the broken armored vehicles
and the tanks,
helicopters,
rats
and plastic pipes.

From the burning horizon they come
accompanied by red winds
and local guides
to bombard again,
with barbarian brotherhood,
the grooves and the holes
and the men whose corpses scattered in the sands.
Then they go away
towards the sunset horizon
behind the vanishing lines.

Helicopters

with ravenous primaries
still move round and round
and their engines are still roaring
spreading in the valleys
their black shrieking.

'Til the End of the World

Oh old summer
creeping on the water
over the grass
and the heart arteries,

let this naked child
replace that tree,
take her scent
beyond the stars,
sink her little feet
in the grassy water,
take her
in your traveling river
under the sun
and under the clouds
and let us oh merciful summer
go with the stream
like reckless waves,
split
and get closed
and run with the waters
till the end of the world.

And you do not know
Sweetness
snoops on a sleepy child
at midnight.

How much I talked to you as a daisy
before you become a clear night!

How much I lost words
when I contemplate
your sleepy eyes!
How much
I covered you with my lasting grieves
and smelled you
and how much I died beside you
yet you do not know.

Portrait

You stand like a tree
and move beneath it
like water.

The Eyes of Foxes

My god,
I am waiting here
but I couldn't enter.

My god,
my hands were working,
my fingers changed their forms,
my breath became white
and my return became impossible.

My god,
I am still looking at you
from a hole

besieging you
by the eyes of the foxes.

In One Kiss

The windows
are the night diamonds
gleaming from far
from a small opening
among the trees.

The windows
are small fountains
walking with us hugging each other.
Coming down the versant with us
in one long kiss.

The windows,
after love
and the extinguish of ecstasy
and the closing of the eyelids,
we hear
their murmur
slipping gently
among the branches.

Lift Me as a Rose

Lift me as a rose
and kiss me.
After a while
I'll close my lids
and you'll never see me.

From Love...From Loneliness

Eagerly I kiss your body
as if I came back from death,
as if I were fire
burning in alcohol drops,
as if I were a scream
coming out of pain
and after the tremor
I cry from torment,
from love
and loneliness.

Let Not the Wolf Enter the Garden of Your House

And I Say Oh Heart

Don't be afraid oh heart, I say.
Sink in water to the bottom,
sink in a deep air
and let ghosts
fight each other
outside.

And I say forget your words
oh heart,
forget the meaning
forget what you meant
forget how much you weigh,
forget the earth and the gravity
and sink in a small drop of water
that swims
in a transparent light.

Wolf

You always say
let not the wolf
enter the garden of your house.
It will lick your wounds
and seek the help of
the hungry moon
beyond the clouds.

Yet,
you did the forbidden
and opened the door to it
using circumstances as an excuse,
you blamed the absent ghost,
the watch that ticked not
that blocked your way
and let the hungry moon
lick your wounds,
and call other wolves
from beyond the clouds.

Artwork by Sadiq Assaieg

About the Author

Sadiq Assaieg was born in Baghdad 1936. He is a poet, cinematographer, plastic artist and critic. He has published four books of poetry: *The Song of Rhinoceros*, *A Country for the Soul*, *Where the Heart Is* and *Wounds of the Old Trees*. He has held four exhibitions of his plastics art. He directed two documentary films for Prague TV in 1984: *An Ordinary Zionism* and *A Clue for the Country*. He adapted the play *Mr Puntila and His Man Matti* by German playwright Bertolt Brecht for the theatre in Baghdad 1978. He currently resides in Baghdad. Email: sadiqart@hotmail.com

---

A good poem is a process of quiet distillation. In this conclusion reside all basic configurations of the human being, the hard and the mysterious, from him thousands of vague references issue and need to be understood and interpreted accurately without elaborating. In fact I hate elaboration even in the classical masterpieces and I cannot find myself there as a reader. I was expelled from these places, and always looking for a place to hide where I feel safe, and nobody asks me to leave it. There I feel like I completed my humanity, and my desire in life renewed and my hope persists to increase to live another life different from the life I live among others."

—Sadiq Assaieg

About the Translator and Editor

Soheil Najm was born in Baghdad in 1956. An internationally known poet and translator, he is the author of *Breaking the Phrase* (Beirut, 1994), *I Am Your Carpenter, Oh Light* (Damascus, 2002) and *No Paradise Outside the Window* (Baghdad, 2008).

Soheil translated *The Gospel According to Jesus Christ* by Jose Saramago and *The Serpent and the Lily* by Nikos Kazantzakis into Arabic. He was the editor of *Gilgamesh*, Iraq's cultural magazine in English and the journal, *Foreign Cullture*, in Arabic. He is now the managing editor of the electronic journal *Irag Literary Review* in English.
Email: soheilnajm@yahoo.com

www.ingramcontent.com/pod-product-compliance
Lightning Source LLC
Chambersburg PA
CBHW071536080526
44588CB00011B/1693